An Old Fashioned Christmas,
Designed and stitched by Karyl Smith,
quilted by Aimee Mahan

FOUR SEASONS AT
MINGLEWOOD

AMERICAN HOLLY
Designed and stitched by Suzanne Earnest,
quilted by Aimee Mahan

Four Seasons at Minglewood

BY DEBBIE ROBERTS

Four Seasons at
Minglewood

By Debbie Roberts

Editor: Deb Rowden

Designer: Brian Grubb

Photography: Aaron T. Leimkuehler

Illustration: Eric Sears

Technical Editor: Christina DeArmond

Production assistance: Jo Ann Groves

Published by:
Kansas City Star Books
1729 Grand Blvd.
Kansas City, Missouri, USA 64108

First edition, first printing
ISBN: 978-1-935362-87-6

Library of Congress Control Number: 2011921878

Printed in the United States of America by Walsworth Publishing Co., Marceline, MO

To order copies, call StarInfo at (816) 234-4636 and say "Books."

 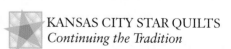

About the Author

Debbie Roberts was born and raised in Papillion, Nebraska. At the time of this writing, she and her husband Don have five children, seven grandchildren and another on the way.

Debbie was a 4-H kid and for as long as she can remember, has loved and worked with fabric. Her many years in 4-H resulted in a love of quilting that developed into her career. While searching for a business she could pursue at home to allow her to be with her family, she became a highly proficient, talented quilter and long-armer. Eventually, Debbie realized it was time to expand her business and opened a quilt store, The Quilted Moose, in 1999. The Moose, as it's known, is located in Gretna, Nebraska, a bedroom community to Omaha, Nebraska. Eventually her shop was featured as a Top 10 Quilt Shop in Quilt Sampler magazine in the fall of 2007. As part of the feature, she designed an original quilt for that article which became the cover quilt for that issue. Debbie's original quilt designs have also been featured in American Patchwork and Quilting, Quilter's Newsletter, and McCalls Quilting magazines, along with quilts in books by Blackbird Designs and Jo Morton.

Recently, Debbie and her husband Don opened Minglewood Lodge as a complement to her quilt business. To read more about the Lodge, see page 10.

Bottom left: Wooden bobbin
German Black Forest needle and thread case
Top right: Antique proddy tool (for rugmaking),
late 19th century

Acknowledgements

Those near and dear to me know this book wouldn't have been possible without their help, understanding and commitment. But each of them deserves public recognition for their ceaseless time and effort. As they say, "If you see a turtle on a fence post, you can be sure he didn't get up there by himself". And so it is with this book.

To Don – Every day and night I thank my lucky stars for such an amazing husband. Thank you for your help with the text, moving and hauling of props for the photo shoot, your patience with my meltdowns and most importantly, your belief that I could do it. If it were not for your love and support, the dream of the Quilted Moose and Minglewood Lodge would not have come true.

To Diane "Rudy" Kabourek – You are my self-professed Computer Goddess. Whether I need an answer to a computer problem or the name for a quilt, you always come through. Our customers have you to thank for taking my handwritten instructions and turning them into logical, easy to follow directions and graphics. Your dry wit and endless good humor always brightens up my day. This book wouldn't have been possible without your time and energy.

To Karyl Smith, Sue Haffke, Cindy Prusa and Suzanne Earnest – It may not take a village to design and stitch a quilt, but it does take a wonderful group of friends. I am so thankful for your collaboration on these projects. Each of the quilts adds your own interpretation and imagination to the theme of this book.

To Christie Lee of Apple Creek Designs – Your Sunset Storms design is a beautiful addition to our seasonal book. Thank you for sharing it with us.

To Cindy Koehlmoos, Suzanne Earnest and Karyl Smith – Thank you for accepting the challenge of creating your own gorgeous versions of our featured quilt.

To Aimee Mahan, Michele Pettorini and Debbi Treusch – You are truly artists who work in thread. Your creative skills bring depth and life to these wonderful quilts.

To Suzanne Earnest and Brenda Reid – Details are always important. Thank you for allowing your treasured notions to be photographed.

To Lance Dunker – I'm sure when you agreed to build Minglewood Lodge you had no idea what was in store. You not only made the dream come true, but you did it with humor, thoughtfulness and an unparallel level of skill. Thank you doesn't seem like enough.

To Mike Anderson – I never met an electrician who lost sleep over getting the job done right. When you said you did, I knew you were the one to shine a light on Minglewood Lodge. Thank you for your ideas and your dedication to this project.

To Aaron Leimkuehler – Although our paths touched for just a day, your wonderful eye for lighting and composition have created photos I will treasure forever.

To Brian Grubb –I am forever in your debt for creating such a beautiful volume. Your vision and design made it all possible.

To Deb Rowden – Every ship needs a captain, every book needs an editor. It is your editing skill that assembled all the pieces into one clear and concise package. You kept me on my toes, you encouraged me, and more than that, you helped me believe that this book could be a reality.

To Diane McLendon and Doug Weaver – Thank you and the Kansas City Star for believing that my concept could become one of your beautiful books. I know you must have latitude to take a leap of faith and I appreciate you made that leap for me.

To Jo Ann Groves – Even the best photographs need production assistance. Thank you for using your eye for detail and color to make these pictures perfect.

To Eric Sears – Your talent to draw perfect diagrams and artwork from my paper templates is remarkable. Thank you.

To Christina DeArmond, my technical editor – Your ability to find those pesky mathematical errors gives me confidence that the instructions and templates are accurate. Thanks for being part of my Kansas City Star team.

Contents

Bottom left:
Paper mache glove darner
Goose wing knitting needle holder
(note the initials are tiny nails)
Top right: Leather hand painted needle book,
early 20th century Sea grass thimble holder

Introduction

I'll be the first to admit that I don't like the cold. When I'm working in my garden and sultry sun is dancing off my SPF 30 skin, I love to simply sit back and soak up the sun, letting the thought of flannel pajamas, hot tea or coffee and a warm quilt become a distant memory. That being said, I am a true mid-westerner in that I love the changing of the seasons and the sights, sounds, and activities that come with each.

We start with spring in the Midwest. After a long, cold winter, we can't wait to get outside again and plant the gardens with flowers and vegetables for a bountiful harvest of both color and sustenance. I've gone from planting gardens with my children to now planting gardens with their children. What was often a solitary endeavor when my kids were in their teens has now become something that resembles a door-buster sale on the day after Thanksgiving! And I love it. Although I confess I still wish my diminutive diggers would stay around for the weeding!

Summer brings hot temperatures. The porch swing calls us to relax in the shade with a glass of cold lemonade. I watch the kids playing in the sprinkler and share their wonderment at everything the outdoors has to offer, including the bugs and creepy-crawly things they invariably find. Mother Nature is at her most colorful as gardens grow and change in the sun. And in the blink of an eye, a storm gathers causing nature's color palette to explode. Our senses are flooded with vibrant hues we can only hope to rival with fabric.

Crisp clear nights, bonfires with marshmallows and the smell of turkey in the oven – it's fall. When the house fills with people to watch a football game, carve a pumpkin, or take pictures of precious little ones in costume, I'm always happy. These are all great excuses for getting together with family and friends. We think back to our own child-hood - remember carving a pumpkin, with mom and dad watching intently to ensure that when it's over, you'll still be able to count to ten without resorting to your toes? Or how excited you were to move from the kid's table to the adult table at Thanksgiving?

That brings us back to the fact that I don't like the cold. But every cloud has a silver lining and winter is no exception. The best part about cold weather is the house filling with sounds and smells connected with this special time of year. The sounds: a child's laughter, parents whispering Christmas secrets, jingle bells, and carols all tumble through space in a harmonious hubbub. What better ways to brighten up a time of year whose real purpose is to make us happy until spring once again arrives?

This book is dedicated to change. As the seasons change, our lives are touched by sights and sounds, colors and feelings making up the patchwork each of us call life. The projects in this book represent a variety of techniques and colors we hope will offer you the opportunity to complement the seasons with an assortment of beautiful quilts.

ABOUT MINGLEWOOD

Quilting, while solitary in some ways, is easily one of the most social of the creative endeavors. Minglewood Lodge came into being with this thought in mind. Situated in a rural part of Sarpy County, Nebraska, the post and beam building evokes the warmth of a Rocky Mountain retreat - yet it is located just minutes from the Quilted Moose.

Minglewood evolved from a happy confluence of unrelated factors. As a longtime quilter, Debbie frequented quilt retreats around the Midwest. The friendships formed and the obvious enjoyment by all the attendees lingered in the back of her mind.

By chance, Debbie was invited to a party celebrating the completion of a friend's post and beam barn. As she looked around the structure, filled with people enjoying the craftsmanship and ambience, it occurred to her that this kind of building would be perfect for a quilting retreat. If done properly, she mused, such a facility with modern conveniences, but built in an old fashioned style, would resonate with those who quilt. So, all that was left was to find the location, design the building, find a general contractor, provide the financing and oversee its completion. No problem.

The right setting was probably the most important factor. It could not be built in the city. It needed a rural locale with the conveniences of a big city nearby. Not an easy task, but Minglewood sits on five acres of prairie with picturesque sunsets framed by the large front porch.

As you enter Minglewood, you are struck by the discernable strength of the structure. The large wooden posts and beams, the massive stone fireplace with cedar log mantle, the hand-forged stair railings, all speak craftsmanship of a time gone by.

When the book was conceived, the obvious choice for the photo shoot was Minglewood Lodge. We hope you enjoy the book and your visual retreat at the lodge.

We've included some helpful hints and some recurring techniques that we will mention throughout the Block of the Month (BOM) series. Please read these instructions before you begin and refer to them often.

Helpful Hints

- All blocks are 12" square finished.
- All seams are a scant 1/4".
- Accuracy is critical so we recommend using a 50 weight thread.
- When instructed to cut a block once diagonally, sub-cut the block once to make 2 half-square triangles.

- When instructed to cut a block cut twice diagonally, sub-cut the block twice to make 4 triangles.

Half-Square Triangle Units

1. Draw a diagonal line on the wrong side of the lighter squares.
2. Putting right sides together, match a lighter color square to a darker color square.
3. Stitch each set of squares a scant 1/4" from each side of the diagonal line.

4. Cut along the diagonal line to make 2 half-square triangles from each set of squares.
5. Press the seam toward the darker side.

Quarter-Square Triangle Units

1. Make half-square triangle units as directed above.
2. Draw a diagonal line on the wrong side of the blocks across the seam.

3. With right sides together, match 2 of the half-square triangle blocks, aligning the seams with opposite colors together.

Top to bottom:
  Flax comb
  Bone carved thread winder
  Darning egg

4. Stitch each set of squares a scant 1/4" from each side of the diagonal line.

5. Cut along diagonal line to make 2 quarter-square triangles from each set of squares.

6. Use the clipping trick (see below), and press the seam toward the darker sides with the intersection open.

Flying Geese Units

1. Draw a diagonal line on the smaller squares.
2. Align 2 of the small squares on opposite corners of the larger square.
3. Stitch a scant 1/4" from each side of the drawn lines.

4. Cut apart on the drawn line and press toward the small triangles.

5. Place one small square on each of the cut pieces and stitch a scant 1/4" from each side of the drawn line.

6. Cut along the drawn line and press toward the smaller unit.

Clipping Trick

1. Clip through both layers of the seam allowance, up to the seam line 1/4" on each side of the seam intersection, shown in the diagrams at the arrows.

2. Press the seam allowances in the direction they need to lay and reduce the layers.

3. Press the center of the intersection open.

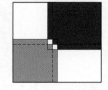

Right top to bottom:
Ivory needleholder, 1820 or earlier
Bone stiletto
Bone thread winder

How we created our Block-of-the-Month Quilt

My friend Suzanne believes everyone should have a Christmas quilt. She has made so many that she now shares them through lectures and trunk shows. My quilt shop, the Quilted Moose, is a great place to find Christmas fabrics: traditional, metallic, contemporary, and whimsical – we carry it all. We have featured many block-of-the-month quilts designed by others, but none seemed to be the Christmas quilt we knew our customers would love.

So we took the plunge and decided to design our own block of the month quilt. We decided it should include lots of traditional blocks to challenge our customers with accurate piecing and assembly - enough to make a bed size quilt without too much other filler.

We chose 10 star blocks and 5 other traditional designs to reach our goal of 15 blocks. We challenged our quiltmakers to complete 2 blocks per month in 2 variations - that way they could explore how differently these blocks could look when colored differently. A good example of this is my Christmas Traditions quilt (page 16). By using these 30 blocks and a center medallion to incorporate my love of appliqué, it generously covers a queen-sized bed.

We then challenged the Quilted Moose staff to create their own quilts made with these blocks, to inspire customers looking for different setting ideas. Starlit Path (page 26), using selected blocks, was one result of this challenge. Moda Fabrics generously supplied their newest French General line, Pom Pom de Paris, for this quilt. You'll find additional designs throughout this book (see pages 1, 2, 59, and 110). Hopefully they will inspire you to find other ways to use our Christmas blocks.

CHRISTMAS TRADITIONS

Designed and stitched by Debbie Roberts
Quilted by Aimee Mahan
Finished quilt size: 101" x 101"

*F*amilies have one thing in common at Christmas –
traditions. Whether you are passing them on or building new
ones, traditions bring us together at the holidays. So what better
way to build a quilt than by using favorite traditional blocks in a
sampler? Tied together with the holly and mistletoe of the season,
15 blocks in varying color combinations are intertwined with
a railed sashing and 9-patch cornerstones to make this elegant
holiday quilt.

Fabric Requirements

COMPLETED BLOCKS - 32
(patterns are on pages 30-73)

Center appliqué background - 1 yard

APPLIQUÉ FABRICS
Assorted greens to equal 1/2 yard
    Assorted reds to equal 1/8 yard
    Assorted golds to equal 1/8 yard
    Brown - 3/8 yard
    Black scraps
9-Patch background - 1/2 yard
9-Patch corners and centers - assorted pieces to equal 1/2 yard
Sashing outer rails - 2-1/2 yards
Sashing center rail - 1-1/4 yards
Outer border and binding - 2-1/2 yards
Backing - 9 yards

FOR THE BLOCKS
Assorted yardage to equal:
Lights = 3 3/4 yd
Reds = 1 1/2 yd
Greens = 1 1/2 yd
Gold = 1/2 yd
Blacks = 1 3/4 yd

Center Appliqué

Use the appliqué layout on page 24 to arrange the small leaves, flower petals and holly leaves (templates on pages 21 – 23).

1. Cut a 30" square from the center appliqué background fabric.
2. Using the large leaf templates on pages 22-23, make 8 center holly leaves.
3. Using the small leaf templates on page 21, make 40 assorted leaves.
4. Using the flower petal templates on page 21, make 4 petals from each template.
5. Make 4 flower centers 1" in diameter using the black fabric.
6. Make 22 berries using the red fabrics, varying the diameters between 5/8", 3/4", and 7/8".
7. Make 3/8" stems from the brown fabric. When doing the appliqué, you will narrow the end to a point.
8. Using the layout as a guide, appliqué all pieces to the background fabric.
9. When the appliqué is completed, trim the block to 27-1/2" x 27-1/2".

Make the 9-Patch Cornerstones

You need a total of 48 cornerstones. Finished cornerstones blocks are 3" x 3".

1. From the 9-Patch background fabric, cut 192 squares 1-1/2" x 1-1/2".

2. From the 9-Patch corners and centers fabric, cut 240 squares 1-1/2" x 1-1/2".

3. Using 4 background squares and 5 corners/centers squares, stitch 9-patch blocks. Press the seams using the clipping trick in the General Instructions, page 12.

Make the Railed Sashing

You need a total of 80 sashing rails.

1. From the sashing outer rails fabric, cut 160 rectangles 1-1/2" x 12-1/2".
2. From the sashing center rail fabric cut 80 rectangles 1-1/2" x 12-1/2".
3. Stitch sashing outer rail rectangles to each long side of a sashing center rail, pressing seams toward the dark rails.

Complete the Quilt

1. Arrange the blocks, the center appliqué block, the sashing, and the cornerstones and stitch into rows.
2. Stitch rows together to form the quilt top.
3. Cut 11 strips 4-1/2" wide x width of fabric from the border fabric and piece together.
4. Cut 2 strips to length of quilt top, and stitch to the sides of the quilt.
5. Cut 2 more strips to width of quilt top and stitch to top and bottom of quilt.
6. Layer the quilt top, batting, and backing and quilt as desired.
7. Cut 11 strips 1-1/4" wide x width of fabric. Piece and bind quilt.

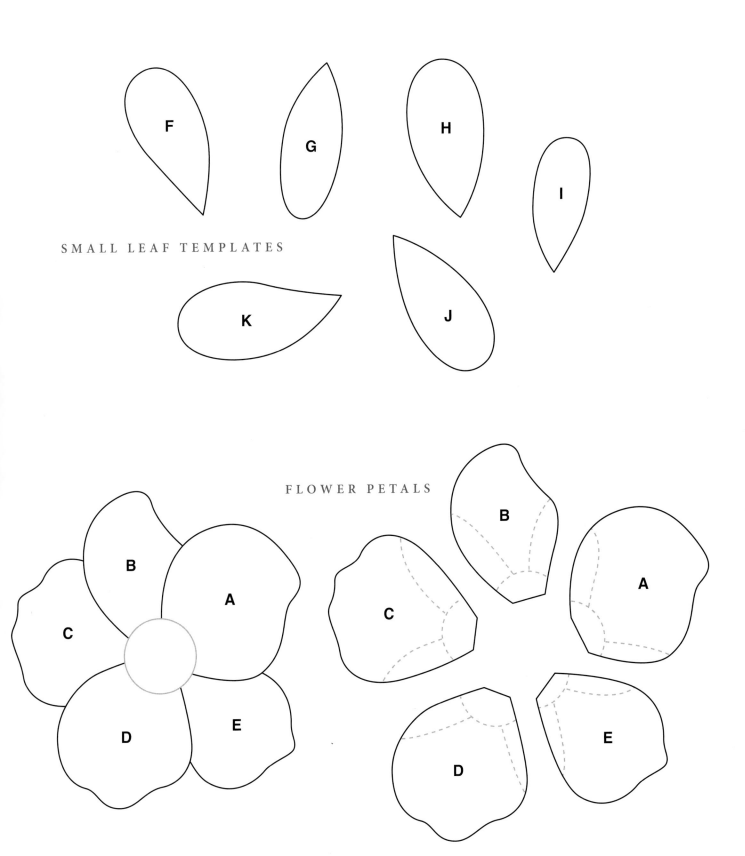

SMALL LEAF TEMPLATES

FLOWER PETALS

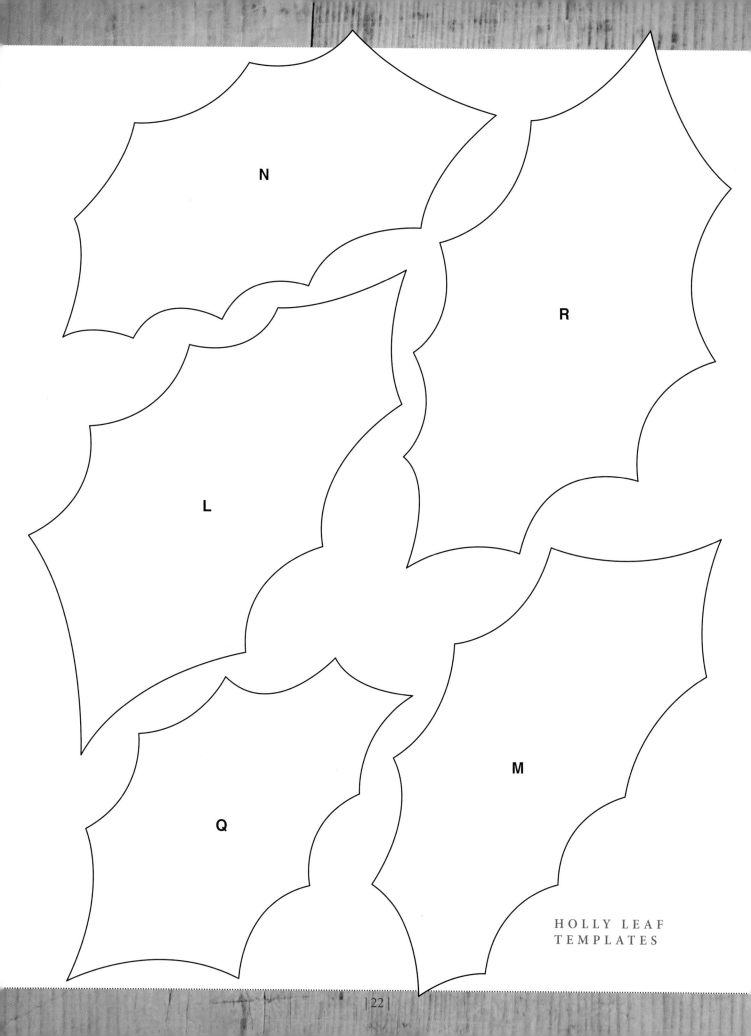

N

R

L

Q

M

HOLLY LEAF
TEMPLATES

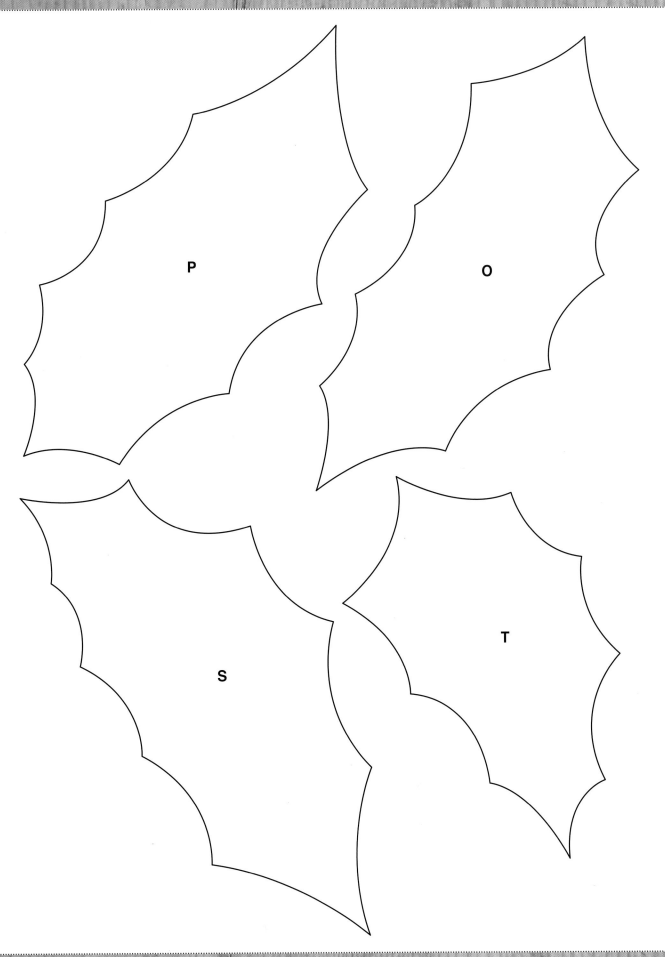

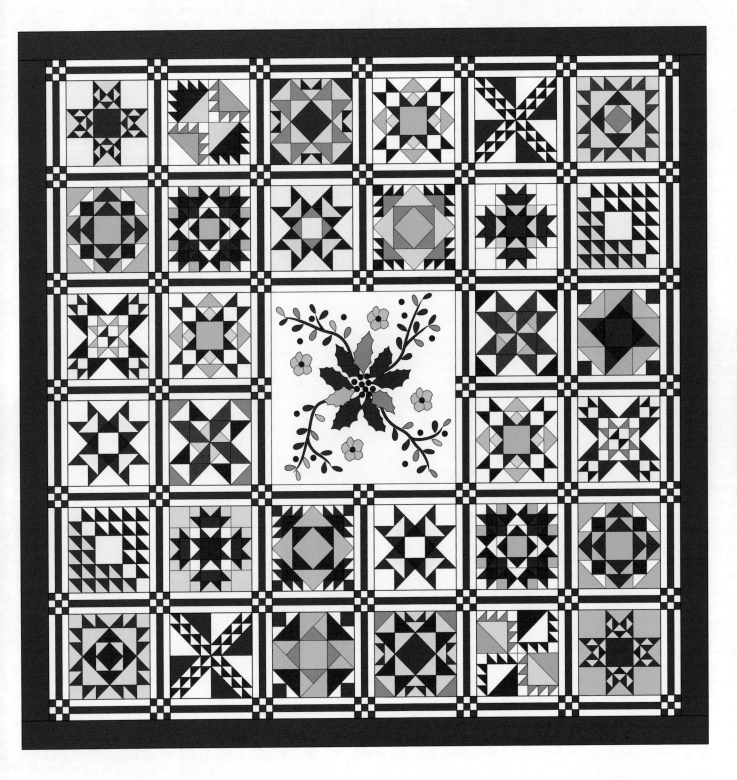

Starlit Path

Designed and stitched by Debbie Roberts
Quilted by Aimee Mahan
Finished quilt size: 76" x 76"

*S*ometimes all it takes is a bit of a color to change the look and feel of a traditional block. *In Starlit Path, we've taken the same traditional blocks used in Christmas Traditions (page 16) and set them in soft colors, reminiscent of a spring evening. Set on point and making use of a striped fabric for the sashing, this quilt evokes a feeling of a formal garden with paths separating each unique flower bed. A floral border completes the effect with the look of a hedge surrounding that garden.*

Fabric Requirements

COMPLETED BLOCKS – 13
(patterns are on pages 30-73)

Sashing - 2-1/4 yards
Setting and corner triangles - 1 yard
Inner (1st) border - 3/8 yard
Middle (2nd) border - 5/8 yard
Outer (3rd) border - 2 yards
Cornerstones - 1/4 yard
Binding - 3/8 yard
Backing - 4-1/2 yards

FOR THE BLOCKS

Assorted yardage to equal:
   5 light fat quarters
   5 yellow fat quarters
   5 pink fat quarters
   5 red fat quarters
   3/4 yard green

Cutting the Sashing, Setting Triangles and Setting Corners

All sashing is cut lengthwise from the fabric.

1. Cut 7 strips 2" wide by the length of the fabric.
   From these strips cut:

      2 of the strips to 69-1/2" long.

      2 of the strips to 42-1/2" long; cut the remaining
      part of the 2 strips to 15-1/2" long.

      The 3 remaining strips into 18 strips 12-1/2" long.

2. Cut 2 squares at 21" x 21" and cut
   twice diagonally for the setting triangles.

3. Cut 2 squares at 12" x 12" and cut once diagonally for
   the setting corners.

Complete the Quilt

1. Referring to the diagram, arrange the blocks, sashing, setting triangles, and corner triangles. Stitch into rows.

2. Stitch rows together to form the quilt top. Setting and corner triangles were cut oversized, so trim the quilt center leaving a 1/4" seam allowance. Quilt top will be 60" x 60", unfinished.

3. Cut 7 strips 1-1/4" wide x width of fabric from the inner border fabric and piece together.

4. Cut 2 inner border strips to length of quilt top, and stitch to the sides of the quilt.

5. Cut 2 inner border strips to width of quilt top and stitch to top and bottom of quilt.

6. Cut 7 strips 2" wide x width of fabric from the middle border fabric and piece together.

7. Cut 2 middle border strips to length of quilt top, and stitch to the sides of the quilt.

8. Cut 2 middle border strips to width of quilt top and stitch to the top and bottom of quilt.

9. Cut 4 strips 6-1/2" wide x length of fabric from the outer border fabric. The unfinished quilt top should now measure 64" x 64".

10. From the cornerstone fabric, cut 4 squares 6-1/2" x 6-1/2".

11. Cut 4 outer border strips to length/width of quilt top (64").

12. Sew 2 outer border strips to the sides of the quilt.

13. Sew cornerstones to each end of the remaining 2 outer border strips. Sew to the top and bottom of quilt.

14. Layer quilt top, batting, and backing and quilt as desired.

15. Cut 8 strips 1-1/4" wide x width of fabric. Piece and bind quilt.

ASSEMBLY DIAGRAM

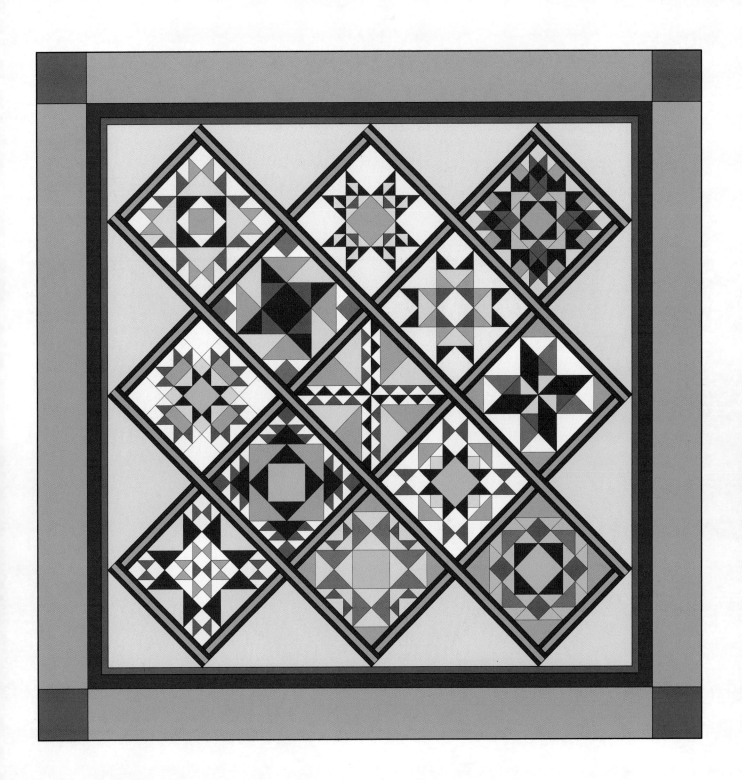

CHRISTMAS TRADITIONS

Arrow Crown

The Blocks

STARLIT PATH

Arrow Crown

Cut

A	2	4-1/4" squares
B	8	2-3/8" squares
C	4	2" squares
D	8	2-3/8" squares
E	4	2" squares
F	1	3-1/2" square
G	8	2" squares
H	3	4-1/4" squares
I	4	2-3/8" squares
J	4	2" squares

Assembly

Note: refer to General Instructions (page 12) to make the units below.

1. Using 4 of the B squares and 1 H square, make flying geese units.
2. Using 4 of the B squares and 4 D squares, make half-square triangle units.
3. Using the remaining 4 D squares and the 4 I squares, make half-square triangle units.
4. Using the remaining 2 H squares and the A squares, make quarter-square triangle units.
5. Following these diagrams, assemble the block.

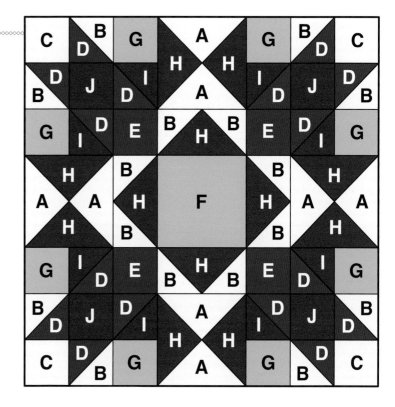

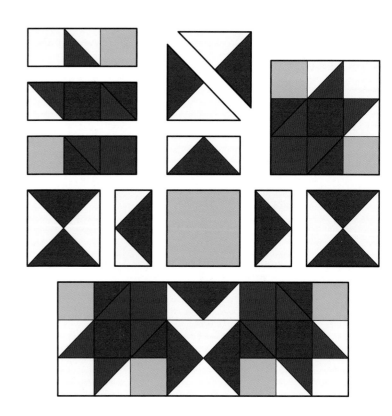

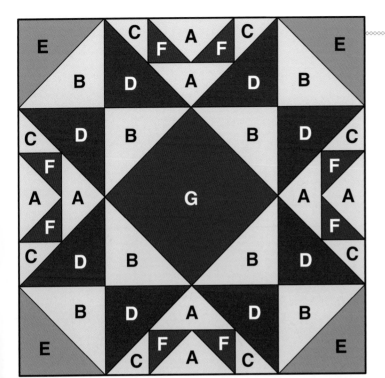

Crow's Foot

Cut

A	2	4-1/4" squares
B	4	3-7/8" squares
C	4	2-3/8" squares, cut once diagonally
D	4	3-7/8" squares, cut once diagonally
E	2	3-7/8" squares
F	4	2-3/8" squares
G	1	4-3/4" square

Assembly

Note: refer to General Instructions (page 12) to make the units below.

1. Using 2 of the B squares and all of the E squares, make half-square triangle units.
2. Using 1 of the A squares and all of the F squares, make flying geese units.
3. Cut the remaining A square twice diagonally.
4. Cut the remaining B squares once diagonally.
5. Following these diagrams, assemble the block.

CHRISTMAS TRADITIONS

Crow's Foot

CHRISTMAS TRADITIONS

Flaming Star

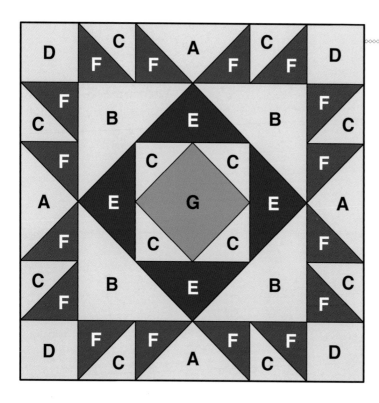

Flaming Star

Cut

A	1	5-1/4" square
C	2	2-7/8" squares, cut once diagonally
C	4	2-7/8" squares
D	4	2-1/2" squares
B	2	4-7/8" squares, cut once diagonally
G	1	3-3/8" square
E	1	5-1/4" square, cut twice diagonally
F	8	2-7/8" squares

Assembly

Note: refer to General Instructions (page 12) to make the units below.

1. Using 4 F squares and the A square, make flying geese units.

2. Using 4 of the C squares and the remaining 4 F squares, make half-square triangle units.

3. Following these diagrams, assemble the block, squaring as follows:

   a. When you have stitched the C triangles to the G block, square the piece to 4-1/2" square.

   b. After you have added the E squares, square the piece to 6-1/8".

   c. After you have added the B squares, square the piece to 8-1/2".

Star and Pinwheels

Cut

A	1	7-1/4" square, cut twice diagonally
B	1	4-1/4" square, cut twice diagonally
C	2	3-7/8" squares
D	1	4-1/4" square, cut twice diagonally
E	4	3-7/8" squares, cut once diagonally
E	2	3-7/8" squares
E	2	3-7/8" squares, cut once diagonally

Assembly

Note: The flying geese units in this block are not constructed as explained in the General Instructions. The points are not the same fabric on each side. Refer to the photo to make those sections.

1. Using the 2 C squares and the 2 E squares, make half-square triangle units as instructed in the General Instructions.

2. Following these diagrams, assemble the block.

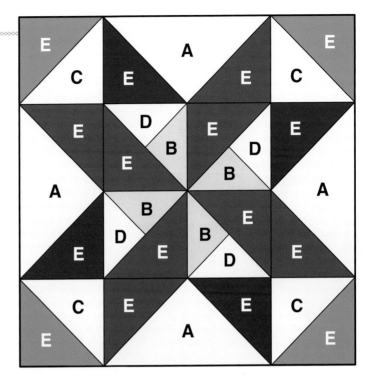

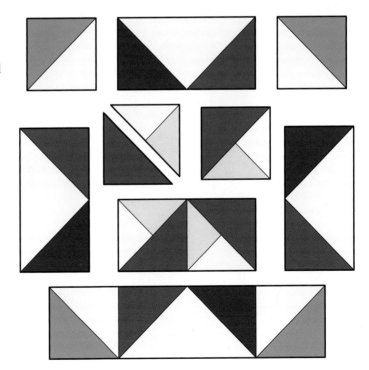

CHRISTMAS TRADITIONS

Star and Pinwheels

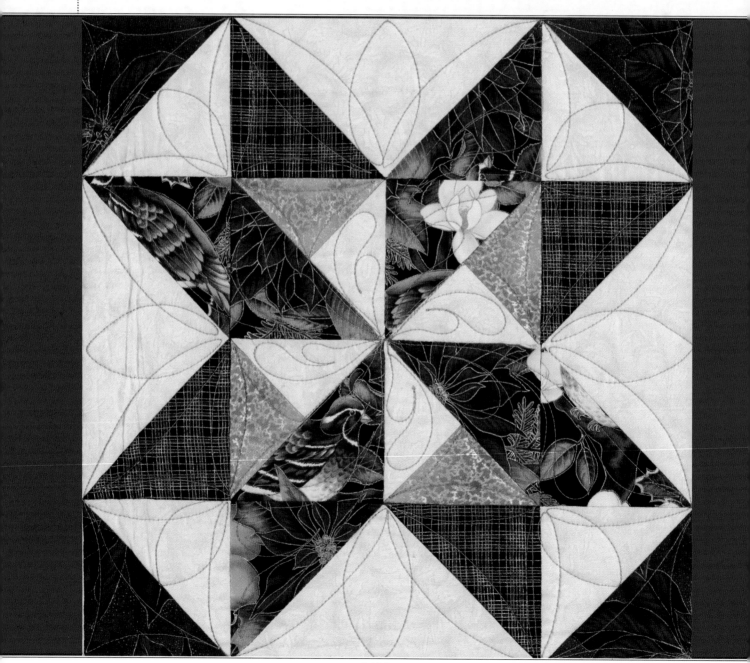

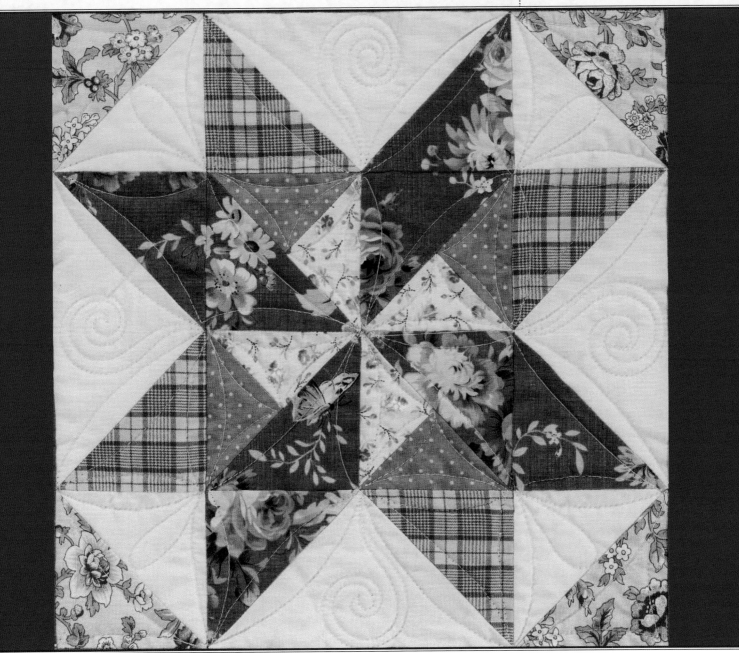

CHRISTMAS TRADITIONS

Kaleidoscope

Kaleidoscope

Cut

A	1	5-1/4" square, cut twice diagonally
B	4	4-1/2" squares
C	2	3-1/4" squares, cut twice diagonally
C	6	2-1/2" squares
D	1	4-1/2" square
E	4	3-1/4" squares, cut twice diagonally
E	6	2-1/2" squares

Assembly

Note: refer to General Instructions (page 12) to make the units below.

1. Using the 6 - 2-1/2" C squares and the 6 - 2-1/2" E squares, make half-square triangle units. Trim to 1-7/8" square.

2. Using 8 of those half-square triangles, stitch an E triangle to each side of the opposite color half of the half-square triangles.

3. Using the remaining 4 half-square triangles, stitch a C triangle to each side of the opposite color half of the half square triangles.

4. Following these diagrams, assemble the block.

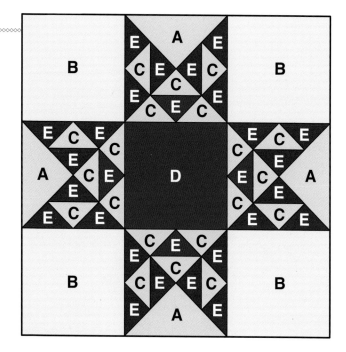

Forest Path • Lawyer's Puzzle

Cut

A	2	5-3/8" squares
B	12	2-3/8" squares
C	4	2" squares
D	2	5-3/8" squares
E	12	2-3/8" squares

Assembly

Note: refer to General Instructions (page 12) to make the units below.

1. Using the B squares and E squares, make half-square triangle units.

2. Using the A squares and D squares, make half-square triangle units.

3. Following one of these 2 layouts, assemble 1 block.

FOREST PATH

LAWYER'S PUZZLE

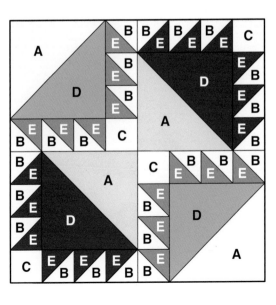
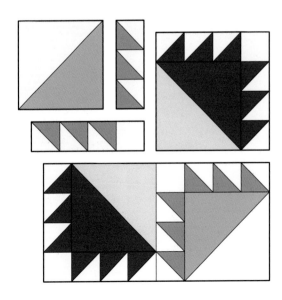

BLOCK 6

FOREST PATH

CHRISTMAS TRADITIONS

Crown Over Star

Crown over Star

Cut

A	2	4-1/4" squares
B	4	3-1/2" squares
C	4	2-3/8" squares
D	12	2" squares
E	1	3-1/2" square
F	4	2-3/8" squares
G	4	2" x 3-1/2" rectangle
H	8	2-3/8" squares

Assembly

Note: refer to General Instructions (page 12) to make the units below.

1. Using the C squares and 4 of the H squares, make half-square triangle units.

2. Using 1 of the A squares and the 4 remaining H squares, make flying geese units.

3. Using the remaining A squares and the 4 F squares, make flying geese units.

4. Following these diagrams, assemble the block.

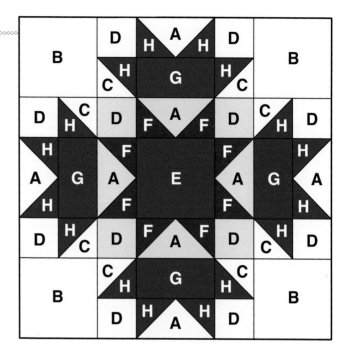

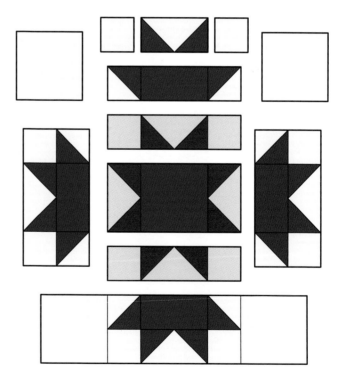

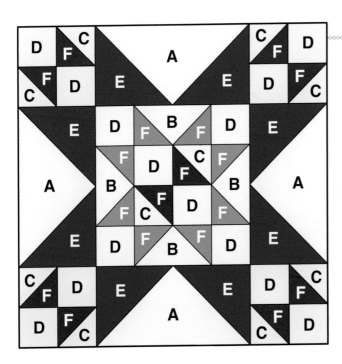

Coronation

Cut

A	1	7-1/4" square
B	1	4-1/4" square
C	5	2-3/8" squares
D	14	2" squares
E	4	3-7/8" squares
F	9	2-3/8" squares

Assembly

Note: refer to General Instructions (page 12) to make the units below.

1. Using the C squares and 5 of the F squares, make half-square triangle units.
2. Using the A squares and E squares, make flying geese units.
3. Using the B square and the remaining F squares, make flying geese units.
4. Following these diagrams, assemble the block.

CHRISTMAS TRADITIONS

Coronation

CHRISTMAS TRADITIONS

Path through the Woods

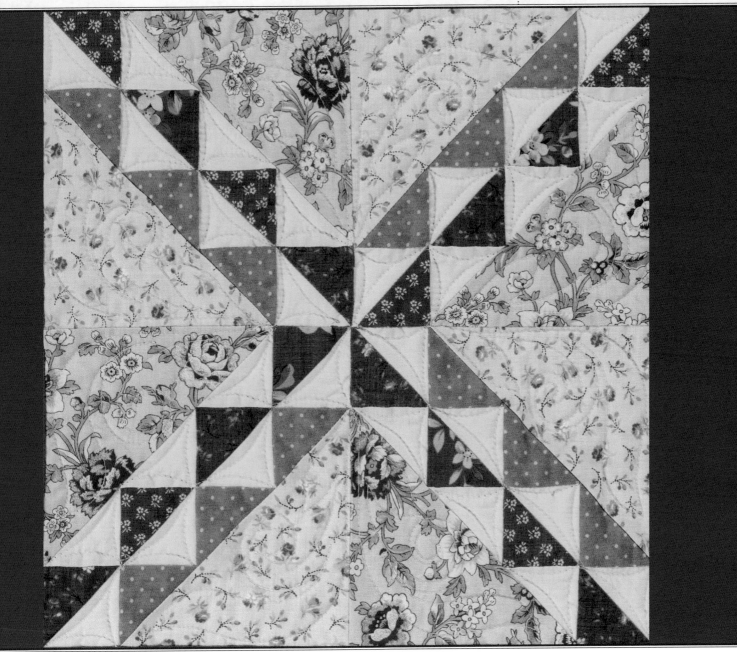

Path through the Woods

Cut

A	2	5-3/8" squares, cut once diagonally
B	8	2-3/8" squares
B	6	2-3/8" squares, cut once diagonally
C	2	5-3/8" squares, cut once diagonally
D	8	2-3/8" squares
D	6	2-3/8" squares, cut once diagonally

Assembly

Note: refer to General Instructions (page 12) to make the units below.

1. Using the 8 B squares and the 8 D squares, make half-square triangle units.

2. Following these diagrams, assemble the block.

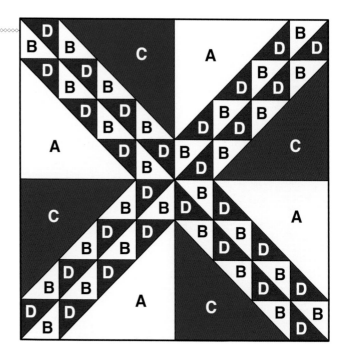

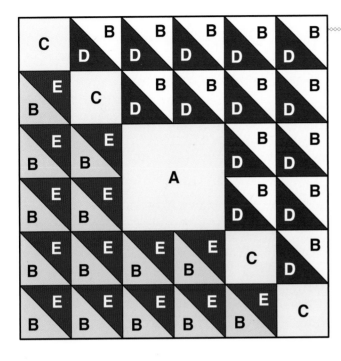

Mosaic Variation

Cut

A	1	4-1/2" square
B	4	6" squares
C	4	2-1/2" squares
D	2	6" squares
E	2	6" squares

Assembly

1. Draw 2 diagonal lines on the wrong side of the 4 B squares.

2. Match 2 of the B squares to the D squares, putting right sides together to make 2 sets of B/D squares.

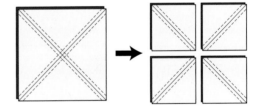

3. Match the remaining B squares to the E squares, putting right sides together to make 2 sets of B/E squares.

4. For each set of squares, stitch a scant 1/4" from both sides of the drawn diagonal lines.

5. Cut each set of squares into 3-1/2" squares as shown above.

6. Cut each square along the drawn diagonal line to make 2 half-square triangles. Trim each to 2-1/2" square.

7. Following these diagrams, assemble the block.

CHRISTMAS TRADITIONS

Mosaic Variation

You'll notice various sampler blocks in other sampler quilts throughout the book. Block 10 also appears in this version, Starlit Christmas Eve, designed and stitched by Cindy Koehlmoos, quilted by Aimee Mahan. the book.

CHRISTMAS TRADITIONS

Double X

Double X

Cut

A	1	7-1/4" square, cut twice diagonally
B1	4	2-3/8" squares, cut once diagonally
B2	2	5" squares
C	2	5" squares
D	4	2" squares
E	1	4-3/4" square
F	4	3-7/8" squares, cut once diagonally

Assembly

1. Draw 2 diagonal lines on the wrong side of the B2 square.
2. Match the B2 square to the C square, putting right sides together.
3. Stitch a scant 1/4" from both sides of the drawn diagonal lines.
4. Cut each into 2-1/2" squares as shown at right.
5. Cut each square along the drawn diagonal line to make 2 half-square triangles. Trim each to 2" square.
6. Following these diagrams, assemble the block.

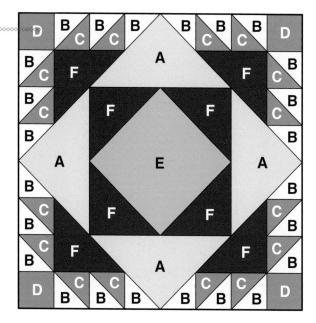

Christmas Star

Cut

A	2	5-1/4" squares, cut twice diagonally
B	1	4-1/2" square
C	2	3-1/4" squares, cut twice diagonally
D	8	2-1/2" squares
E	1	5-1/4" square, cut twice diagonally
F	4	1-7/8" squares
G	8	2-7/8" squares, cut once diagonally

Assembly

1. Following these diagrams, assemble the block.

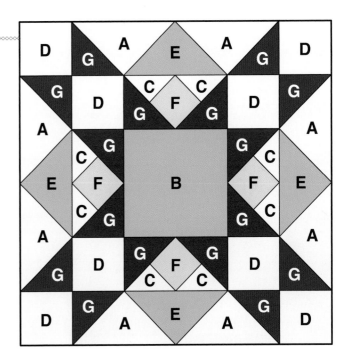

CHRISTMAS TRADITIONS

Christmas Star

CHRISTMAS TRADITIONS

King's Crown Squared

King's Crown Squared

Cut

A	8	2-7/8" squares
B	1	4-1/2" square
C	4	2-7/8" squares, cut once diagonally
D	2	5-1/4" squares
E	2	4-7/8" squares, cut once diagonally
F	4	2-1/2" squares

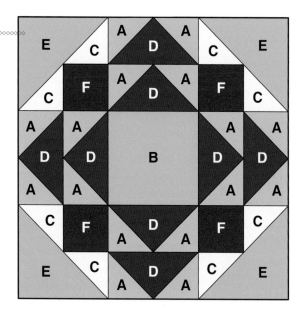

Assembly

Note: refer to General Instructions (page 12) to make the units below.

1. Using the A squares and the D squares, make flying geese units.

2. Following these diagrams, assemble the block.

Broken Star

Cut

A	1	7-1/4" square, cut twice diagonally
C	5	3-1/2" squares
B	2	3-7/8" squares, cut once diagonally
D	2	4-1/4" squares, cut twice diagonally
E	2	4-1/4" squares, cut twice diagonally
F	1	4-1/4" square, cut twice diagonally

Assembly

1. Following these diagrams, assemble the block.

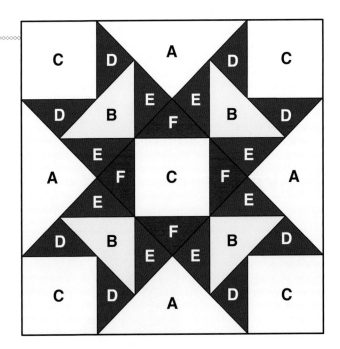

CHRISTMAS TRADITIONS

Broken Star

Cut

A	1	5-1/4" square, cut twice diagonally
B	2	4-7/8" squares, cut once diagonally
C	1	4-1/2" square
D	4	2-7/8" squares, cut once diagonally
E	1	5-1/4" square, cut twice diagonally
F	2	4-7/8" squares, cut once diagonally
G	4	2-1/2" squares

CHRISTMAS TRADITIONS

Aunt Dinah

Assembly

1.   Following these diagrams, assemble the block.

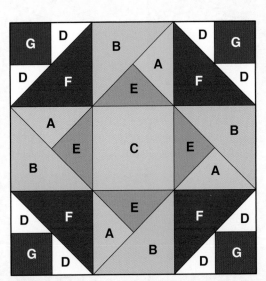

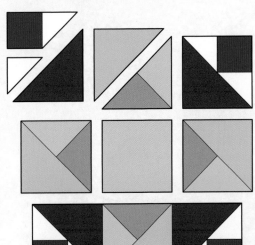

STARLIT PATH

FOUR SEASONS OF QUILTS

TREASURES OF MINGLEWOOD

Carved needle case

Hand-carved bone basket from India, 1800-1820

Ivory sewing bird, 1820 or earlier

FLORABUNDANCE

Designed by Sue Haffke and Debbie Roberts, stitched by Sue Haffke
Quilted by Aimee Mahan
Finished quilt size: 55" x 55"

*H*ow glorious are the warm days of spring? We revel in the chance to get out of the house without a coat and start planning gardens for the coming season. Those first blooms of spring are popping their heads out and you know the days will be filled with new color. By May Day, the kids will be able to pick their favorites for baskets to give family and friends. A dance around the maypole comes to mind with Florabundance. It's circle of flowers and ribbon sashing complete with an inner scalloped border makes this quilt just right for your May Day celebration!

Fabric Requirements

Background - 1-3/8 yards
Dark sashing - 1/4 yard
Appliqué flowers - 1/2 yard
Appliqué leaves and stems - 1/2 yard
Reverse appliqué in flower - 1/4 yard
Appliqué (scalloped) border - 1-1/4 yards
Outer border - 1-1/2 yards
Binding - 1/4 yard
Backing - 3-1/2 yards

Appliqué Blocks

Use the appliqué templates (see page 82-83).

1. Cut 4 squares 20" x 20" from the background fabric.
2. Cut appliqué flowers, leaves, stems, and reverse appliqué, using the templates provided, from the appliqué fabrics.
3. Appliqué the flowers with the reverse appliqué, leaves and stems to the background squares using your favorite appliqué method.
4. Trim squares to 18-1/2", centering the appliqué in the block.

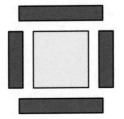 

Sashing

1. Cut 1 square 2-1/2" x 2-1/2" from the background fabric.
2. Cut 2 rectangles 1" x 2-1/2" from the dark sashing fabric.
3. Cut 2 rectangles 1" x 3-1/2" from the dark sashing fabric.
4. Using the square and rectangles, sew a Courthouse Step block as shown at right.
5. Cut 4 strips 2-1/2" x 18-1/2" from the background fabric.
6. Cut 8 strips 1" x 18-1/2" from the dark sashing fabric.
7. Sew a dark sashing strip to each lengthwise edge of the background fabric strips as shown at below. You will have 4 pieced units.

Complete the Quilt Top

1. Using the appliquéd squares and 2 of the pieced sashing units, sew 2 rows of appliqué squares and sashing, referring to the diagram.

2. Using the Courthouse Step square and the remaining pieced sashing units, sew 1 one sashing row.

3. Sew the 3 rows together, using the Assembly Diagram on page 80 for the direction of the flowers and stems.
4. Cut 4 lengthwise strips 8-1/2" x 39-1/2" from the outer border fabric.
5. Cut 4 squares 8-1/2" x 8-1/2" from the outer border fabric.
6. Cut 4 lengthwise scalloped pieces, using the appliqué border template on page 81, from the appliqué border fabric.

7. Cut 4 corner pieces, using the appliqué border corner template, from the appliqué border fabric.
8. Appliqué the scalloped border to the outer border strips and cornerstone blocks.
9. Sew an appliquéd border strip to each side of the quilt.
10. Sew appliquéd cornerstone blocks to each end of the remaining border strips and sew to top and bottom of quilt.
11. Layer the quilt top, batting, and backing and quilt as desired.
12. Cut 6 strips 1-1/4" wide x width of fabric. Piece and bind quilt.

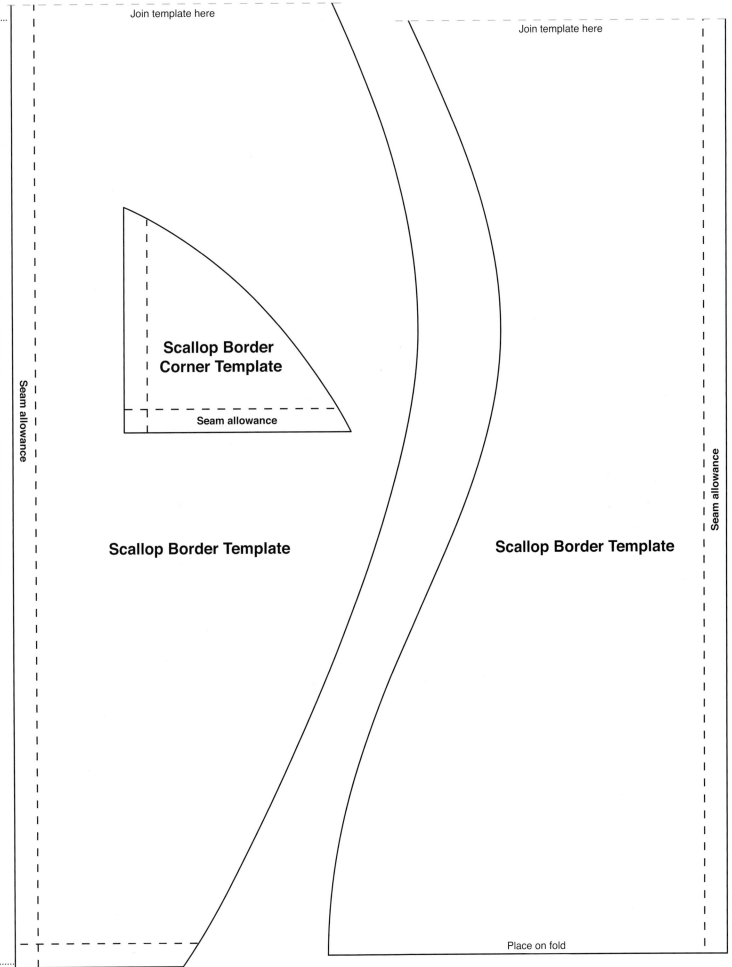

Join template here

Join template here

Seam allowance

Seam allowance

**Scallop Border
Corner Template**

Seam allowance

Scallop Border Template

Scallop Border Template

Place on fold

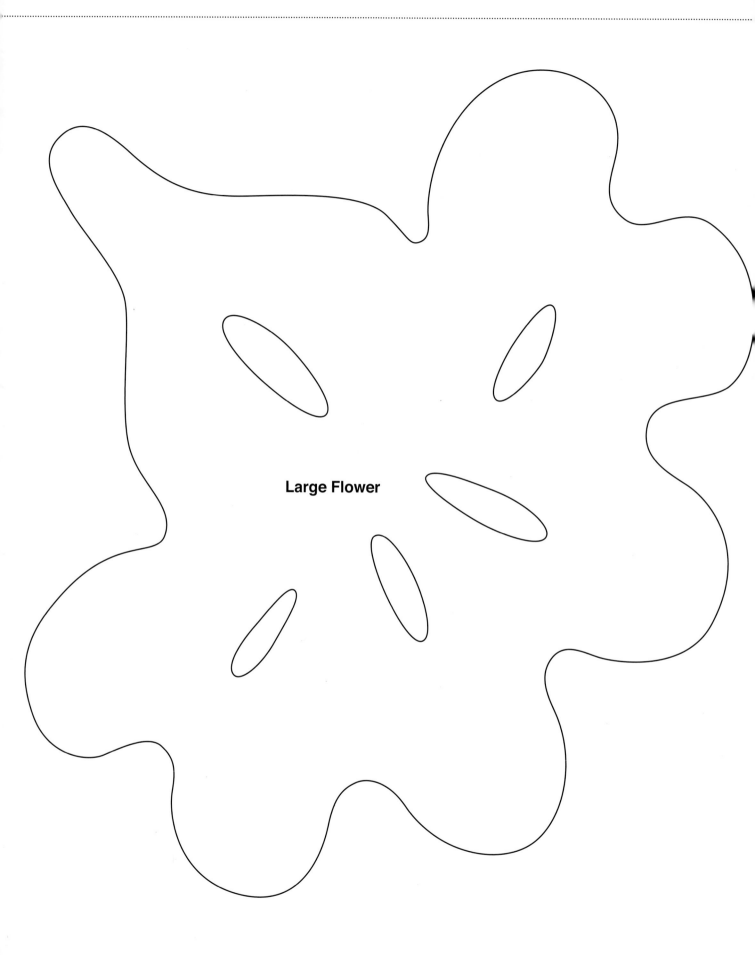

Large Flower

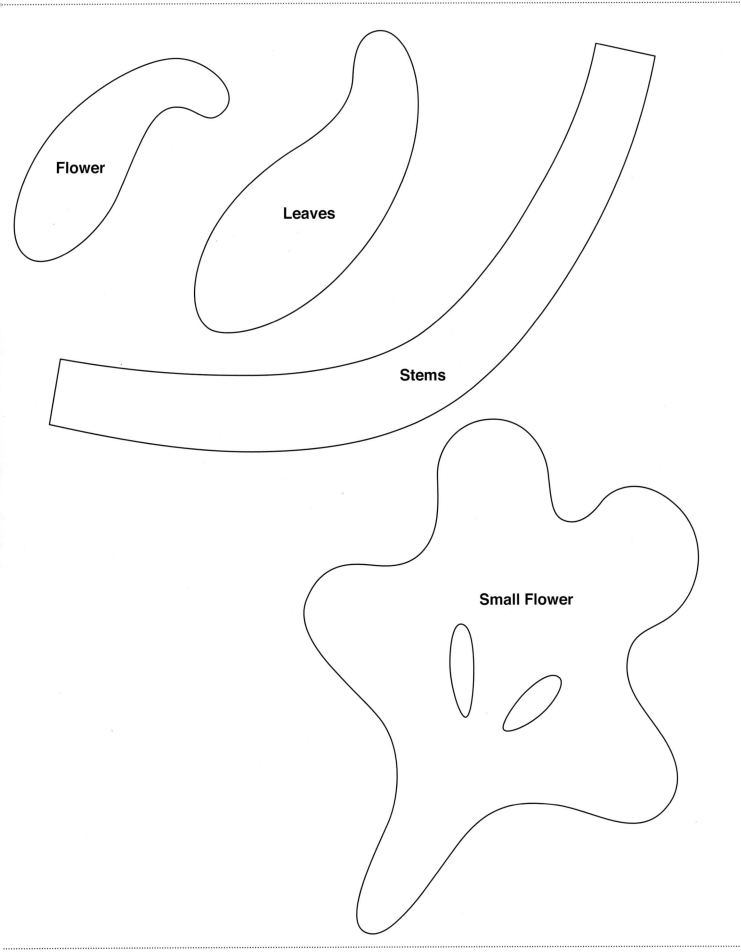

Flower

Leaves

Stems

Small Flower

PORCH SWINGS AND LEMONADE

Designed by Karyl Smith and Debbie Roberts,
stitched by Karyl Smith
Quilted by Debbi Treusch
Finished quilt size: 76-1/2" x 76-1/2"

*T*he kids are out of school and heading for the pool; vacation plans are underway. Summer is here! As the days get hotter, a lazy afternoon on the porch swing with a book is just the ticket to slow things down. By brightening up the colors of a traditional quilt design and using color-washed batiks, this summer quilt is perfect for throwing on that porch swing. A bright sawtooth border reminds us to get out a few lemons and make pitcher of lemonade!

Fabric Requirements

Star points and pieced border background -
    1 yard cream fabric
Star points backgrounds, Star corners and centers, Star
    frame corners, and pieced border - 2-1/2 yards total
    assorted medium and dark fabrics
Alternate blocks and Star frame rectangles -
    3-1/2 yards light fabric
Inner border - 5/8 yard
Outer border - 5/8 yard
Binding - 1/2 yard
Backing - 4-3/4 yards

TREASURES OF MINGLEWOOD

Vegetable ivory thimble holder

Friendship Star Blocks

You will make a total of 41 Friendship Star blocks. The blocks finish at 7-1/2" square.

FOR EACH BLOCK:

1. Cut 2 squares 2-1/2" x 2-1/2" from the Star points fabric.

2. Cut 2 squares 2-1/2" x 2-1/2" from the Star points background fabric.

3. Cut 5 squares 2" x 2" from the Star corners and centers fabric.

4. Using the same fabric from Step 3 above, cut 4 squares 2" x 2" for the Star frame corners.

5. Cut 4 rectangles 2' x 5" from the Star frame rectangle fabric.

6. Using the Star points squares and Star points background squares, make half-square triangle units (see General Instructions, page 8). Square to 2".

7. Following the diagram at right, assemble the Friendship Star block. The block should be 8" square.

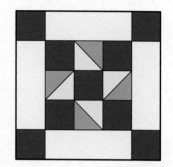

Complete the Quilt Top Center

1. Cut 40 squares 8" x 8" from the alternate block fabric.

2. Using 5 Friendship Star blocks and 4 alternate blocks for each row, stitch 5 rows as shown below and press seams toward the alternate blocks.

3. Using 4 Friendship Star blocks and 5 alternate blocks for each row, stitch 4 rows as shown below and press seams toward the alternate blocks.

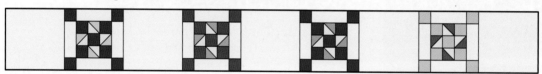

4. Stitch the rows together to complete the quilt top center, alternating the rows just stitched and starting and ending with the rows from Step 2. The quilt top center should now measure 68" x 68".

Inner Border

1. Cut 8 strips 2" wide x the width of the fabric from the inner border fabric. Piece the strips together.

2. Measure the length of the quilt and cut 2 strips to that length. Stitch to the sides of the quilt top.

3. Measure the width of the quilt and cut 2 strips to that length. Stitch to the tops and bottom of the quilt top.

Pieced Border

1. Cut 94 squares 2-1/2" x 2-1/2" from the pieced border background fabric.

2. Cut 94 squares 2-1/2" x 2-1/2" from the pieced border fabrics.

3. Using these squares, make half-square triangle units (see General Instructions, page 12) for a total of 188 half-square triangles units. Square each to 2".

TREASURES OF MINGLEWOOD

Vegetable ivory hand carved needle and thimble holder

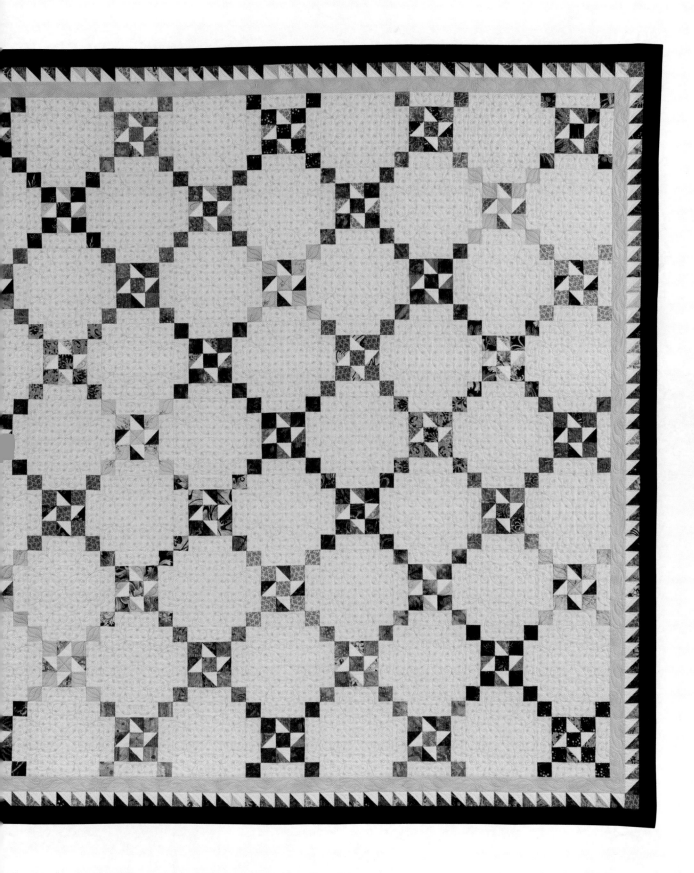

4. Cut 4 squares 2" x 2" from the pieced border fabrics for the corner blocks.

5. Stitch 4 rows of 47 half-square triangle units, with all the blocks facing the same direction.

6. To 2 of the border rows, stitch a corner block on each end.

Outer Border

1. Cut 8 strips 2" wide x the width of the fabric from the outer border fabric. Piece strips together.

2. Measure the length of the quilt and cut 2 strips to that length. Stitch to the sides of the quilt top.

3. Measure the width of the quilt and cut 2 strips to that length. Stitch to the tops and bottom of the quilt top.

Complete the Quilt

1. Layer quilt top, batting, and backing and quilt as desired.

2. Cut 9 strips 1-1/4" wide x width of fabric. Piece and bind the quilt.

ASSEMBLY DIAGRAM

SUNSET STORMS

Designed and stitched by Christie Lee
Quilted by Aimee Mahan
Finished quilt size: 34" x 39"

*S*ummer storms are a way of life here. Days are hot and humid and around sunset, dark clouds often gather forecasting the advancing storm. The contrast of those clouds against the rich colors of the summer sunset is awe-inspiring. Then you see a flash of light and find yourself counting, just like you did when you were little to gauge how quickly you would hear the crack of thunder. This quilt captures the drama of a thunderstorm by using stormy blues and grays together with the vibrant colors of a sunset. It finishes with a border of summer flowers nourished by the rain.

Fabric Requirements

4 medium fabrics for blocks (corners and flying geese in Block 1) – 1/4 yard each
5 dark fabrics for blocks (corners and centers for Block 2 and flying geese points in Block 1) – 1/4 yard each
5 light fabrics for block centers (Block 1) – scraps to equal 1/4 yard total
5 medium fabrics for blocks (triangle points in Block 2) – scraps to equal 1/4 yard total
Setting and corner triangles – 1/4 yard
Inner border – 1/4 yard
Outer border – 2/3 yard
Binding – 1/3 yard
Backing – 1-1/4 yard

Cutting Instructions

BLOCK 1
Note: Repeat to make 20 blocks total.
Cut 1 – 2-1/2" square of light fabric for center.
Cut 4 – 1-1/2" squares of medium fabric for corners.
Cut 1 – 3-1/4" square of medium fabric for flying geese.
Cut 4 – 1-7/8" squares of dark fabric for flying geese.

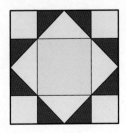

TREASURES OF
MINGLEWOOD

Ivory hand carved tape measure

BLOCK 2

Note: Repeat to make 12 blocks total.

Cut 1 – 3-3/8" squares of dark fabric for centers.

Cut 4 – 1-1/2" of dark squares for corners.

Cut 4 – 1-7/8" medium squares. Cut each square in half once diagonally.

Setting and Corner Triangles

Cut 4 – 6 7/8" squares from medium fabric. Cut each square twice diagonally for a total of 16 side setting triangles. (2 of the triangles will not be used for this quilt.)

Cut 2 – 3-3/4" squares from medium fabric. Cut each square in half once diagonally for the corner triangles.

Inner Border

Cut 2 – 1 1/4" x 28 3/4" strips for sides.

Cut 2 – 1 1/4" x 24 1/2" strip for top and bottom.

Outer Border

Cut 2 – 5" x 30 1/4" strips for sides.

Cut 2 – 5" x 33 1/2" strips for top and bottom.

TREASURES OF MINGLEWOOD

Pewter thread and thimble holder

Block 1 Assembly

1. Draw a diagonal line on back of all 1 7/8" dark squares with a fine- point marking tool.

2. Using the 1 7/8" dark squares and the 3 1/4" medium squares, make 80 flying geese units (see General Instructions, page 12). Press and trim to 1 1/2" x 2 1/2" for each unit.

3. Sew 4 matching medium flying geese, 4 matching medium 1 1/2" squares and 1 light center into block. Press.

4. Repeat this process with the other light squares, dark squares and flying geese units - make 20 blocks. Blocks measure 4 1/2" square unfinished.

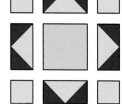

Block 2 Assembly

1. Sew 2 medium triangles on either side of a 1 1/2" dark square. Repeat this with 6 other matching medium triangles and 3 matchingdark squares for a total of 4 corner units. Press.

2. Sew the 4 corner units around a 3 1/4" square. Press.

3. Repeat this process with the other 11 dark center squares and medium triangles - make 12 blocks. Blocks measure 4 1/2" square unfinished.

Quilt Assembly

1. Sew diagonal rows together of alternating blocks with setting triangles. Press.
2. Join rows together and press.

Inner Border

1. Sew long inner border strips to sides of joined blocks. Press toward borders.
2. Sew inner border to ends of quilt. Press.

Outer Border

1. Sew long outer border strips to length of quilt. Press.
2. Sew outer border to ends of quilt. Press.

ASSEMBLY
DIAGRAM

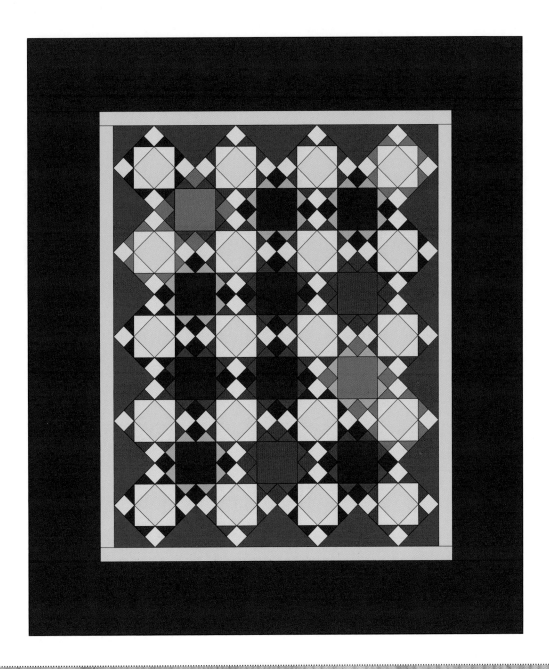

Stars Over Minglewood

FALL

Designed by Cindy Prusa and Debbie Roberts, stitched by Cindy Prusa
Quilted by Debbi Treusch
Finished quilt size: 63" x 63"

Crisp fall evenings are made for bonfires and stargazing. The crackling fires send orange and gold messengers up into the night adding what looks like even more stars to an already full sky. Out here at Minglewood Lodge, the lights of the city are so far away that the night sky sparkles like diamonds and a falling star gives you a chance to make a wish. It seemed only right to have a quilt sprinkled with star blocks and a wide sashing reminiscent of the barn doors at the Lodge. Stitch this quilt for someone you love.

Fabric Requirements

Star points - 1 yard total assorted fabrics
Star centers - 1/3 yard total of assorted fabrics
Star background and sashing - 3 yards
Block centers - 1/4 yard
Block sashing and outer border - 2 yards
Binding - 3/8 yard
Backing - 4 yards

Star Units

You will make 52 stars. The finished size of the Star unit is 4-1/2". For each star unit:

1. Cut 2 squares 2-3/4" x 2-3/4" from the Star points fabric.

2. Cut 2 squares 2-3/4" x 2-3/4" from the Star background fabric.

3. Using the star point and background squares, make 4 quarter-square triangle units (see General Instructions, page 12).

4. Cut 1 square 2" x 2" square from the Star centers fabric.

5. Cut 4 squares 2" x 2" from the Star background fabric for the corner squares of the star.

6. Following the diagram at right, assemble the star unit. Press seams toward the solid squares and use the clipping trick (see General Instructions, page 12) the rows are stitched together.

Cut the Border Strips

1. Cut 2 lengthwise strips 5" x 54-1/2" for the side outer borders.

2. Cut 2 lengthwise strips 5" x 63-1/2" for the top and bottom outer borders.

3. Set these strips aside to be used later in completing the quilt.

Sashed Star Block

You will make a total of 9 blocks. The finished size of the Star unit is 12". For each sashed star block:

1. Cut 4 rectangles 3-1/2" x 5" from the block sashing fabric.

2. Cut 1 square 3-1/2" x 3-1/2" from the block centers fabric.

3. Following the diagram at right, assemble the rows for the Sashed Star block, pressing the seams on the top and bottom row toward the sashing blocks and the center row seams away from the center block.

4. Sew the rows together matching the intersections. Press seams toward the center sashing row. The unfinished blocks should measure 12-1/2" x 12-1/2".

Complete the Quilt

1. Cut 24 rectangles 5" x 12-1/2" for the sashing.

2. Stitch 4 rows of 4 star units and 3 sashing rectangles, pressing seams toward the sashing.

3. Stitch 3 rows of 4 sashing rectangles and 3 Sashed Star blocks, pressing the seams toward the sashing.

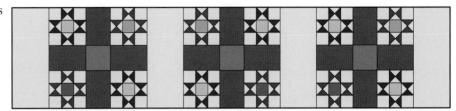

4. Following the Assembly Diagram, stitch the rows together, starting and ending with a narrow row.

5. Stitch 5" x 54-1/2" border strips cut earlier to sides of quilt top.

6. Stitch 5" x 63-1/2" border strips cut earlier to top and bottom of quilt top.

7. Layer the quilt top, batting, and backing and quilt as desired.

8. Cut 7 strips 1-1/4" wide x width of fabric. Piece and bind quilt.

ASSEMBLY
DIAGRAM

ESCAPING THE FROST

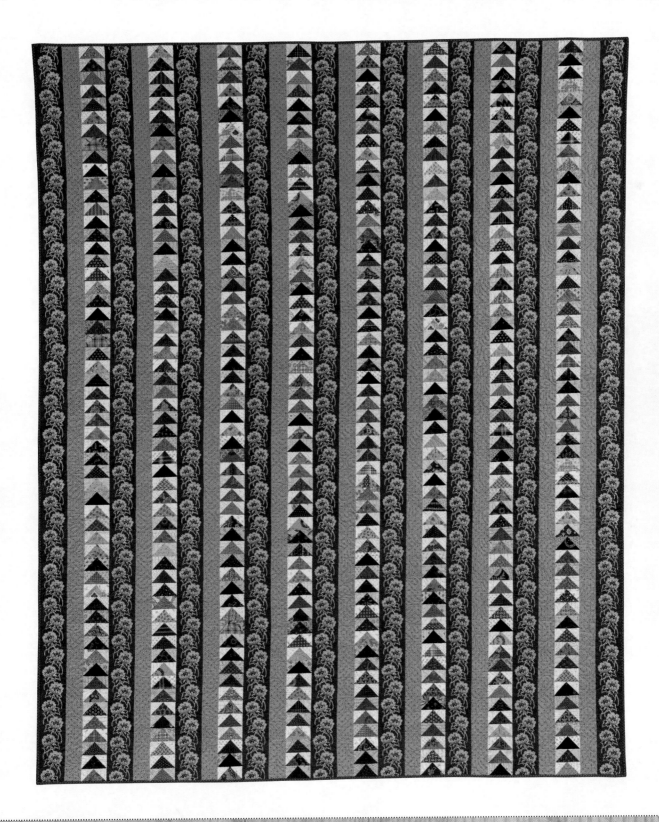

ESCAPING THE FROST

Designed by Suzanne Earnest and Debbie Roberts, stitched by Suzanne Earnest
Quilted by Debbie Roberts
Finished quilt size: 69" x 84"

*O*nce the cool fall weather arrives, the Midwest is filled with geese heading south. *They gather in freshly harvested fields to refuel then, full and rested, they take off in formation to continue their journey. This quilt captures their migration with flying geese units set in rows along side two contrasting strips, mimicking the parallel lines of the farmer's empty fields.*

Fabric Requirements

Geese centers - 2 yards total of assorted medium and dark fabrics
Geese corners - 3 yards total of assorted light and medium fabrics
Light sashing - 2-1/2 yards*
Dark sashing - 2-1/2 yards*
Single-fold binding - 1/2 yard
Backing - 5 yards
Note: if you are using a lengthwise stripe, you may need 5 yards for 9 custom cut strips. Determine how many strips you can cut from one length of fabric and purchase additional 2-1/2 yard lengths if necessary.

Flying Geese Strips

You will make a total of 448 flying geese.

1. From the geese centers fabrics, cut 112 squares 4-1/4" x 4-1/4".
2. From the geese corners fabrics, cut 448 squares 2-3/8" x 2-3/8".
3. Using the geese centers and corners, make flying geese units (see General Instructions, page 12).
4. Assemble 8 rows of 56 geese all pointing the same direction. The completed strips should be 84-1/2" in length.

Note: Assemble the geese strips in sub-sets of 8-10 geese to control the curving of the strips, then stitch the sub-sets together.

Sashing Strips

1. From the light sashing fabric, cut 9 strips lengthwise 2-1/2" wide x 84-1/2" long.
2. From the dark sashing fabric, cut 9 strips lengthwise 3-1/2" wide x 84-1/2" long.

Note: If you are using a lengthwise stripe, you will need to adjust the width of the strips and fussy cut them from the striped fabric.

Complete the Quilt

1. Make 8 strip sets of (left to right) a dark strip, a light strip, and a flying geese strip.

2. Make 1 strip set of (left to right) a light strip and a dark strip.

3. Stitch the 8 flying geese strip sets together with the dark strip on the left.

4. Stitch the light/dark strip set to the right edge of the quilt top, matching the light strip to the flying geese strip so you end up with a dark strip along each lengthwise edge.

5. Layer the quilt top, batting, and backing and quilt as desired.

6. Cut 8 strips 1-1/4" wide x width of fabric. Piece and bind quilt.

ASSEMBLY
DIAGRAM

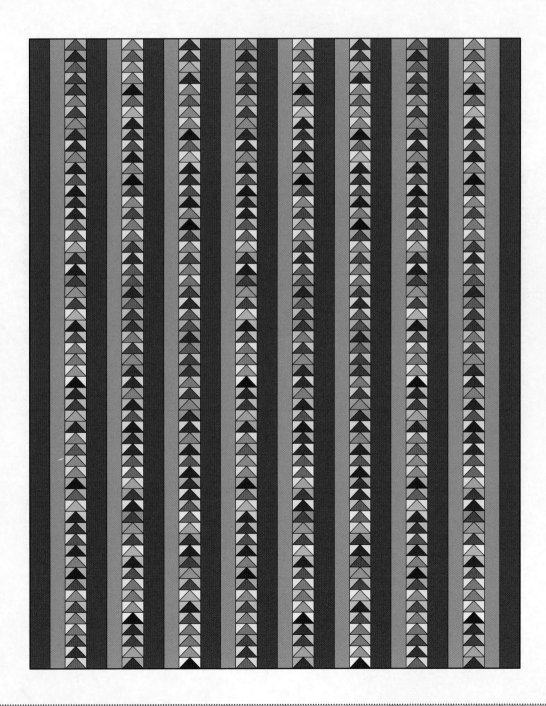

TURKEY DANCE

Designed and stitched by Debbie Roberts
Quilted by Michele Pettorini
Finished quilt size: 39-1/2" x 39-1/2"

*T*ake a drive through the Midwest countryside and you are likely to spot wild turkeys. They waddle and gobble through the fields picking at the grains and seeds left behind after the harvest. Traveling in flocks of anywhere from a few to a few dozen, they are quite the sight! This gathering inspired a quilt of appliquéd turkey tracks organized into a fanciful square dance setting. To corral these turkeys, a border of 9-Patch blocks is the perfect finish.

Materials

Background for blocks and 9-Patches - 1-3/4 yards
Appliqué - 3/4 yard
9-Patch squares - assorted scraps totaling 3/8 yard
Backing - 1 1/4 yards
Binding - 1/4 yard

Appliqué Blocks

You need a total of 16 appliqué blocks. To make each block:

1. Cut:
1	7" squares of background fabric
1	Appliqué center
4	Large leaves
8	Small leaves

2. Mark a 6" square in the center of the background square to help center the appliqué.

3. Using your favorite appliqué method, appliqué all the pieces to the background fabric.

4. Square the block to 6-1/2" square.

TREASURES OF
MINGLEWOOD
*Seashell pincushion on a
sterling silver base, mid 19th
century*

Complete the Quilt Center

1. Cut 9 squares 6-1/2" x 6-1/2" for the alternate blocks.
2. Cut the setting triangles:

   3   10" squares, cut twice diagonally for setting triangles.

   2   5-1/2" squares cut once diagonally for corner setting triangles.
3. Using the setting triangles, corner setting triangles, alternate blocks, and appliqué blocks to stitch the rows of the quilt, referring to the diagram at right for placement.
4. Stitch the rows together to complete the quilt center, again referring to the diagram at right.
5. Trim quilt center, leaving a 1/4" seam allowance.

Make the 9-Patch Blocks

You need a total of 52 - 9-Patch blocks.
To make each block:

1. Cut: 1   1" squares of dark fabric for the center block

   4   1-1/4" squares of dark fabric for the block corners

   4   1" by 1-1/4" rectangles of background fabric
2. Stitch block together, using the clipping trick in General Instructions (page 12) after the rows are stitched together. The blocks should be 2-1/2" square.

Make the Border and Complete the Quilt

1. Cut the setting triangles:

   24   4-1/2" squares, cut twice diagonally for setting triangles

   8   2-3/4" squares cut once diagonally for corner setting triangles

   Note: Setting and corner triangles are oversize to allow for trimming. When 9-patch borders are complete, trim leaving a 1/4" seam allowance.

2. Make 2 borders with 12 of the 9-patch blocks in each, along with setting and corner triangles. Stitch to the sides of the quilt top.

3. Make 2 borders with 14 of the 9-patch blocks in each, along with setting and corner triangles. Stitch to the top and bottom of the quilt top.

4. Layer the quilt top, batting, and backing. Quilt as desired.

5. Cut 5 strips 1-1/4" wide x width of fabric. Piece and bind quilt.

ASSEMBLY
DIAGRAM

TURKEY DANCE TEMPLATES

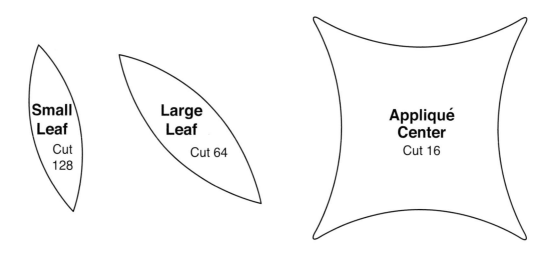

Small Leaf
Cut 128

Large Leaf
Cut 64

Appliqué Center
Cut 16

Two of a Kind Tablerunner

WINTER

*N*othing's more fun on a cold winter night than a friendly game of cards, and you'll need two-of-a-kind to open in our game. The two-of-a-kind in this tablerunner is one of our individual blocks - did you recognize the Coronation block? Duplicate one element of a block like the corner butterfly square and you have a new look. When you add setting triangles and a small border, two 12" squares become an easy tablerunner and a winner in any game.

Designed, stitched
and quilted by
Suzanne Earnest
Finished size:
22-1/2" x 39-1/2"

Fabric Requirements

Background - 1/4 yard
Gold - 1/4 yard
Black - 1/4 yard
Red - 1/4 yard
Pine needles - 1/4 yard
Setting triangles - 1/2 yard
Border and single-fold binding - 1/2 yard
Backing - 3/4 yard
Setting Triangles - 1/2 yard

Cutting

A	2	7-1/4" square background fabric
B	2	4-1/4" square gold fabric
C	12	2-3/8" squares pine needles fabric
D	24	2" squares pine needles fabric
E	8	3-7/8" squares red fabric
F	20	2-3/8" squares black fabric
G	8	2" squares gold fabric

Assembly

1. Using the C squares and 12 of the F squares, make half-square triangle units (see General Instructions, page 12).

2. Using the A squares and E squares, make flying geese units (see General Instructions, page 12).

3. Using the B square and the remaining F squares, make flying geese units.

4. Following the diagram below, assemble 2 blocks. There will be will be 2 extra C/D/F center units, set aside.

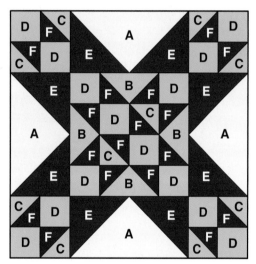

Setting Triangles

1. For the setting triangles, from the background fabric cut:
   2 strips 3-1/2" x 10"
   1 square 14" x 14" cut twice diagonally
   (only 2 of the triangles will be used)

2. Using the 2 completed blocks, the 2 extra C/D/F units, and the pieces just cut, stitch the center of the quilt block together. Trim the corners of the strips off as indicated by the dotted lines on the diagram.

Border

1. From the border fabric cut:
   4 strips 2-1/2" x 18"
   2 strips 2-1/2" x 16"

2. Stitch 2 of the 18" strips to the sides of the quilt top and trim the ends.

3. Stitch the 2 - 16" strips to the diagonal sides and trim (as shown by the dotted line).

4. Stitch the remaining 2 - 18" strips to the last sides and trim (as shown by the dotted line).

16" strips

16" strips

Finishing

Layer quilt top, batting, and backing and quilt as desired. Cut 3 strips 1-1/4" wide x width of fabric. Piece and bind.

HOLLY STARS
Designed and stitched by Suzanne Earnest, quilted by Aimee Mahan

RESOURCES

The Quilted Moose
109 Enterprise Drive
Gretna, Neb. 68028
402-332-4178
headmoose@quiltedmooseonline.com
www.quiltedmooseonline.com

Minglewood Lodge
10603 South 237th Street
Gretna, Neb. 68028
402-332-4178
www.minglewoodlodge.com

Quilters
Aimee Mahan
Splendid Stitches
aimee@splendidstitches.com
Omaha, Neb.

Michele Pettorini
Michele Pettorini Custom Quilting
Michelesquilting.com
515-274-8877
Urbandale, Iowa

Debbi Treusch
Brook Run Quiltworks
515-556-6991
Des Moines, Iowa

Christie Lee
Apple Creek Quilts
402-880-5153
Papillion, Neb.